THE SELF-PUBLISHED WOMAN

www.ingramcontent.com/pod-product-compliance
Lightning Source LLC
Chambersburg PA
CBHW070344130626
46556CB00007B/3030
* 9 7 9 8 9 8 8 9 7 1 7 9 5 *